Get **more** out of libraries

Please return or renew this item by the last date shown.

You can renew online at www.hants.gov.uk/library

Or by phoning 0845 603 5631

 Hampshire
County Council

C015835983

What Does Dead Mean?

A Book for Young Children TO HELP EXPLAIN DEATH AND DYING

Caroline Jay AND Jenni Thomas

ILLUSTRATED BY UNITY-JOY DALE

Jessica Kingsley *Publishers*
London and Philadelphia

First published in 2013
by Jessica Kingsley Publishers
116 Pentonville Road
London N1 9JB, UK
and
400 Market Street, Suite 400
Philadelphia, PA 19106, USA

www.jkp.com

Library of Congress Cataloging in Publication Data
Jay, Caroline, 1953-
  What does dead mean? : a book for young children to help explain death and dying
/ Caroline Jay and Jenni Thomas ; illustrated by Unity-Joy Dale.
    pages cm
  ISBN 978-1-84905-355-6 (alk. paper)
 1. Death--Juvenile literature. I. Thomas, Jennifer Anne, 1943- II. Dale, Unity-Joy, illustrator. III. Title.
  BF789.D4.J39 2012
  155.9'37--dc23
                                 2012032515

British Library Cataloguing in Publication Data
A CIP catalogue record for this book is available from the British Library

ISBN 978 1 84905 355 6
eISBN 978 0 85700 705 6

Printed and bound in China

Dedicated to Laura, Roy and Miles,
whose deaths have shaped our lives.

Our grateful thanks to Nick and Kara Lawson,
founders of the Angus Lawson Memorial Trust,
for their support, and to all the children
whose questions have inspired this book.

THE **ANGUS LAWSON**
MEMORIAL TRUST

The idea for this book came from
the questions children have asked about
what happens when someone dies.

Dear Adults and Children

This book is for you to read together to help talk about what happens when someone dies. It has been written with the understanding that people have very many different beliefs within our multicultural world.

Would you like to try drawing
or painting what you think...?

'What does dead mean?'

When a person dies, they are no longer alive and it means that their body doesn't work anymore. A dead person doesn't run or play or laugh or cry or breathe. Dead people don't need to eat or sleep or keep warm because their bodies don't work anymore.

What do you think dead means...?

'What do dead people look like?'

When a person dies, they may look different from how we remember them. Their body may look pale and it won't move at all. Dead people don't move because their bodies don't work anymore.

What do you think dead looks like...?

'Is being dead like sleeping?'

No, being dead is not like sleeping.

When we are alive, we need to sleep because sleeping helps our bodies to work well and store up energy for the next day.

Sometimes grown-ups say people who are dead have gone to sleep, which is confusing. When we go to sleep, we wake up in the morning. People who die are not asleep and they don't wake up.

What do you think being dead is like...?

'Why can't doctors and nurses make people better?'

Doctors and nurses do everything they can to make people better. Most of the time when people go to the doctor or to hospital they do get better, but sometimes they don't and sometimes they die.

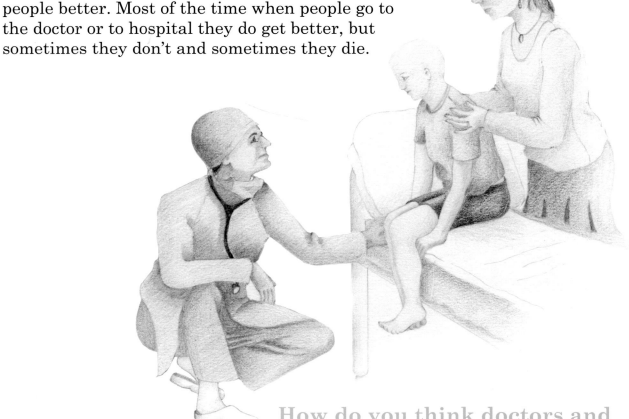

How do you think doctors and nurses can help people...?

'Does dying hurt...?'

When people are dying, they are given medicine to help them not feel pain.

After someone has died, they don't feel pain because their body has stopped working. This is why doctors and nurses don't need to give them any more medicine.

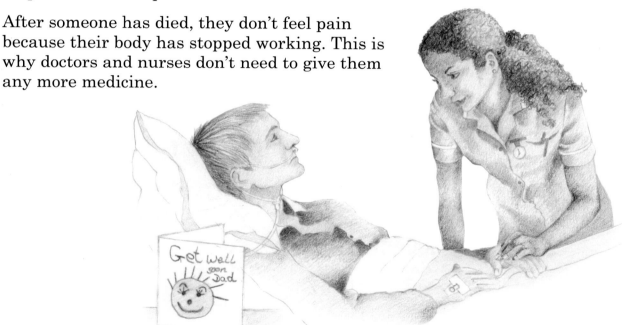

What do you think...?

'Why do babies and children die?'

No one ever expects babies or children to
die but sometimes they do. Babies and
children die for lots of different
reasons. Mostly they get better
when they have been very ill.

What do you
think...?

'Will I die?'

Yes, one day we will all die,
but dying isn't like a cold
– you can't catch it.

You won't
die because
someone you
know has died.

Most people die
when they are old.

Do you know anyone who's died...?

'Why do people have to die?'

People usually die when they're old or very ill or have had a really bad accident. Animals also die.

Doctors can't always make people better and vets can't always make animals better, although they do everything they can.

Have you had a pet that's died…?

'Why did someone I love have to die?'

When someone you love dies, it's very sad. We don't know why, but sometimes things happen to people and they die before they get old.

If you are thinking about why someone you love has had to die, you are not the only one to have these thoughts. There are children in different countries all over the world thinking and perhaps asking the same question.

What are you thinking and asking...?

'Is it someone's fault?'

No, usually it's not anyone's fault when someone dies.
Sometimes children wonder if it was something they did or
thought that made the person die. Nothing anyone says or thinks, however
horrid, can make someone die.

What do you wonder about...?

'Will I ever see the person who's died again?'

We never see the person who's died again here on earth because they can't come back to life. We can sometimes see their dead body at the hospital or funeral directors. Some people believe they will see the dead person again in heaven after they have also died, but nobody knows for sure. Although we can't see the person again here on earth, we can always remember the things we did with them, how they looked and what they said or did. Maybe a sound or smell will remind us of them.

These special things we remember about them are memories which are ours to keep forever.

What do you remember...?

'What's a funeral and can children go?'

A funeral is when family and friends meet to remember the person who's died.

A funeral is usually held in a church, a synagogue or a mosque, depending on the family's beliefs. Words may be said about the person who's died, people may sing, chant, say prayers or read something special.

The dead person's body is usually there, in a box called a coffin, and flowers are sometimes put on the coffin.

Some children decide they want to go to the funeral; others decide they don't. There is no right or wrong thing to do. It helps when grown-ups explain to children what to expect.

Often people will meet after the funeral for something to eat or drink and to share memories about the person who's died.

What do you think...?

'What happens to the person's body at the funeral?'

When a person dies, it's important that we treat their dead body with care. As well as being the time when family and friends meet to remember the person who's died, a funeral is also the time when the person's body is either buried or cremated. Before the funeral the family decide which one it is going to be.

If it's a burial, the dead body is put in a coffin and buried in the ground in a special place, often called a cemetery. Earth is put on top of the coffin and people think of this as the body being mixed with the earth.

If it's a cremation, the dead body is put in a coffin and then into a type of fire that turns it into ashes that can be scattered on the ground or in the wind. People sometimes think of this as the body's ashes being mixed with the air.

If we go to a cemetery, we see headstones that families have put there to mark a special place in memory of the person who's died and been buried there. At a crematorium, plaques can be put up or perhaps a rose planted to remember the person who's died and been cremated there.

How would you like to remember
someone who's died...?

'Where do dead people go?'

We know that dead bodies are buried or cremated. What we have left are all the things we remember about them that made them who they were.

People often think of this part of a person as their soul or spirit. Some people believe that a person's soul or spirit is always around to love and support them. Some people believe that a person's soul or spirit goes to heaven.

Others believe that dead people don't go anywhere, and that when you die there is nothing more.

Different people believe different things. No one knows for sure.

What do you believe...?

'Where's heaven and how do you get there?'

Nobody knows for
sure where heaven is or what it is.

Some people don't believe there is a heaven.

Some people believe heaven is in the sky or in the stars
or in nature like a beautiful sunset.

One thing we do know is that it isn't a place we can get to in
a car or on a bus or a train or a plane.

What do you think about heaven...?

'Will I always have feelings about
the person who's died?'

We usually have feelings about the person who's died. These feelings are called grief.

We may have lots of different feelings. We may feel sad, cross, lonely, scared, worried or even have no feelings at all, like being numb.

Sometimes we may feel bad because we remember things we didn't like about the person who's died.

Everyone is different. Feelings are never right or wrong – they are just how we feel. It's what we do with our feelings that can be good or bad.

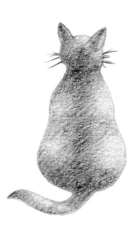

What are your feelings...?

'What can help to let feelings out?'

When we feel upset, there are lots of things we can do to let our feelings out.

- Hugging someone or something can help and be a comfort.

- Doing something physical like running or kicking a ball can help us let feelings out.

- Choosing some flowers or a shrub or a tree to plant in memory of the person who's died.

- Playing a favourite song and dancing – it's OK to be happy and laugh and have fun after someone's died.

- Choosing pictures of the person who's died and making a scrapbook to remember things about them.

• Visiting a place we like going to.

• Telling a friend how we feel –
they might feel the same and
we can share feelings.

• Collecting things that remind us of
the person who's died and making
a Memory Box to put the things in.

• Having a look at some websites with an
adult – there are some on the next page.

• Drawing or painting something
while thinking about the person
who's died, and maybe putting
the picture in a Memory Box.

Here are some useful organisations and websites you might like to look at:

RD4U, part of Cruse Bereavement Care
www.rd4u.org.uk
www.crusebereavementcare.org.uk

Winston's Wish
www.winstonswish.org.uk

The Angus Lawson Memorial Trust
www.almt.org

Seeds of Hope Children's Garden
www.seedsofhopechildrensgarden.co.uk

The Child Bereavement Charity
www.childbereavement.org.uk

Rainbows
www.rainbows.org

Kids Aid
www.kidsaid.com

The National Centre for Childhood Grief
www.childhoodgrief.org.au

Rosie's Rainbow Fund
www.rosiesrainbowfund.co.uk

UK Sands
www.uk-sands.org

The Compassionate Friends
www.tcf.org.uk

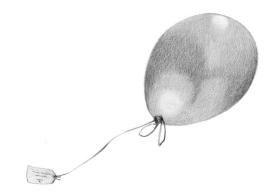